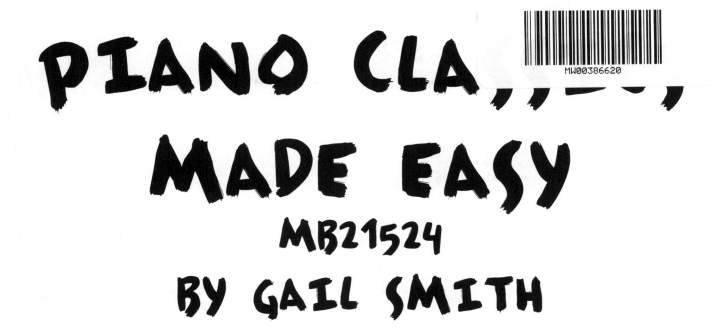

PIANO CLASSICS
MADE EASY
MB21524
BY GAIL SMITH

BILL'S
MUSIC
SHELF

Table of Contents

Foreword

The classical pieces in this collection are favorites the world over. Now it is possible for the beginning piano student to play the classics in an easy, playable rendition that will sound great. Each piece in this collection catches the essence of the composer's original masterpiece and makes it as easy as possible to play.

It is my hope that the student will be inspired to keep playing the piano and practicing until some day they can play the real, original version of the piano solo as Bach, Chopin, Mozart, Beethoven and the other composers originally composed them.

Enjoy!

Gail Smith

Für Elise

Beethoven
Arr. by Gail Smith

4

Mozart's Theme

Arr. by Gail Smith

Spring Song

Vivaldi
Arr. by Gail Smith

Musette

J.S.Bach
Arr. by Gail Smith

Ecossaise

Beethoven
Arr. by Gail Smith

Theme from the Magic Flute

Mozart
Arr. by Gail Smith

Minuet in F

Mozart
Arr. by Gail Smith

Aria from Figaro

Mozart
Arr. by Gail Smith

The Blue Danube

Johann Strauss
Arr. by Gail Smith

March from 'The Nutcracker Suite'

Tchaikovsky
Arr. by Gail Smith

Jesu, Joy of Man's Desiring

J.S. Bach
Arr. by Gail Smith

Pachelbel's Canon

Arr. by Gail Smith

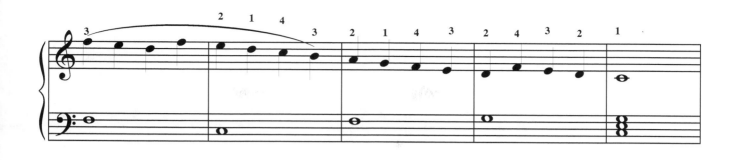

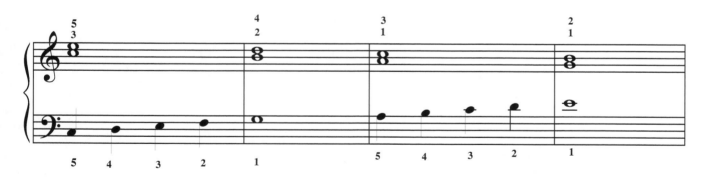

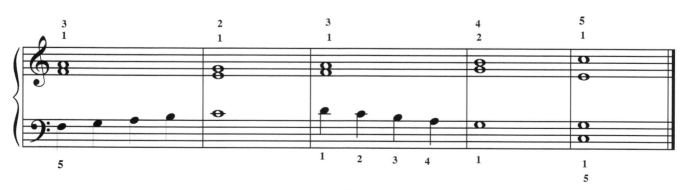

17

Theme from Night Music

Mozart
Arr. by Gail Smith

Nocturne Theme

Chopin
Arr. by Gail Smith

Prelude

Chopin
Arr. by Gail Smith

Theme from Clair de Lune

Claude Debussy
Arr. by Gail Smith

21

Prelude

Chopin
Arr. by Gail Smith

Andante

Symphony Theme

Mozart
Arr. by Gail Smith

Allegro

Rage over a Lost Penny

Beethoven
Arr. by Gail Smith

Allegro

Theme from Moonlight Sonata

Beethoven
Arr. by Gail Smith

Moderato

UNIQUELY INTERESTING MUSIC !